Privie - Toilet

Puling - Whining

Quatch - Tubby

Reechy - Fowl

Shoon - Shoes

Soft you! - Wait!

T'was - It was

Unthrifty - Unlucky

Wherefore - Why

Wot - Know

Yarely - Smart

Roman
Over 2,000 years ago

Viking
Over 1,000 years ago

Junks
Over 1,000 years ago

Carrack
Over 700 years ago

Ships through history

Ferdinand Magellan was a Portuguese captain who became the first person in history known to sail around the entire world. His circumnavigation, undertaken on behalf of Spain, began in 1519 and ended in 1522. His brave adventure aided in proving that the earth is round and not flat, like people once believed.

EARLY LIFE FOR FERDINAND

Ferdinand was born to nobility, but his parents sadly passed away when he was only a boy. Orphaned, he was given the job of being a page to the Portuguese queen. In return for his work, he was taught valuable skills, such as horseback riding, hunting, and sword fighting.

INTRODUCTION TO THE SEAS . . .

In 1505, Ferdinand enlisted in the fleet of Francisco de Almeida and took part in an expedition from the king to fight Muslims along the African and Indian coasts and to create a strong Portuguese presence in the Indian Ocean. Ferdinand learned a lot about sailing and made a name for himself. As years went on, he became a captain. He had become sure that if you sailed far enough west, you'd reach the Spice Islands, but he needed funding to prove his claim. The Portuguese king refused the adventure, so he suggested it to the Spanish king. King Charles V was far more willing and funded Ferdinand.

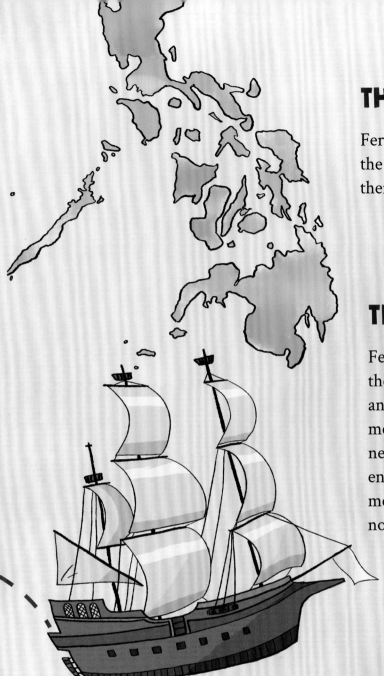

THE FAMOUS JOURNEY

Ferdinand wanted to find a western route between Spain and the Spice Islands to make transporting spices easier. Until then, they'd been sailing around Africa to get there.

THE SHIP AND FLEET

Ferdinand was given five ships: the Trinidad, the Santiago, the Victoria, the Concepción, and the San Antonio, as well as a crew of 270 men. The trip was harrowing; the sailors nearly starved, and there was a mutiny! In the end, only one ship—the Victoria—and 18 crew members survived the whole trip, Ferdinand not included.

THE END OF FERDINAND

Ferdinand never personally completed his circumnavigation of the earth. He was killed in a battle with a native tribe on the island of Mactan.

Decades passed and no one tried to follow in his footsteps, considering the journey too dangerous!
That is, until 55 years later when out set the REAL main character of this story . . .

The book is dedicated to my brilliant mum and dad. Ana also to Kayleigh.

—Farren Phillips

It is NOT dedicated to my old school teachers who said I doodled too much to ever be successful. It seems that you underestimated my annoying persistance to turn doodling into a career!

This Book
Belongs To

- - - - - - - - - -

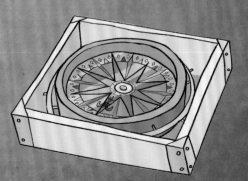

Published by Yeehoo Press
6540 Lusk Blvd, Ste C152, San Diego, CA 92121
www.yeehoopress.com

Edited by Zhiqiao Wang
Designed by Si Ye
Proofread by Amanda McFarlane, Sarah Jane Abbott, and Veronica Scott
Original concept by Luyang Xue and Zhiqiao Wang

Library of Congress Control Number: 2021942337
ISBN: 978-1-953458-34-6
Printed in China First Edition
1 2 3 4 5 6 7 8 9 10

THE SECOND IN THE WORLD

to Sail the Globe: *Sir Francis Drake*

By Farren Phillips

YEEHOO PRESS

Contents

THE DRAKE FAMILY

In the 16th century, England was under the rule of the Tudor dynasty. Francis Drake was born between 1540 and 1544 (no one is sure!). As a kid, Francis loved the ocean and desperately wanted to be a sailor. He was the oldest of 12 boys in his family.

Back in those days, people tended to have lots more children than they do now. This was because life was more dangerous than it is today; they didn't have the kind of medicines we have now, so a lot of children got sick very easily and passed away. Parents would have as many kids as possible to have the best chance of some surviving into adulthood. Many farm families would have especially large numbers of children so that they could help work in the fields. Imagine having that many brothers to bicker with. I've got a headache just thinking about it.

HOME LIFE IN THE 16TH CENTURY

Francis and his family had been living in a place called Crowndale Farm in Devon, which had belonged to his ancestors for over 100 years! They lived in a stone farmhouse, and the boys would have been put to work on the farm as young as five, and they likely all would have been sharing one bedroom, too! Francis was later sent to his Uncle Hawkins in Plymouth. This was the first step in his journey to becoming a sailor.

Farmhouses were attached to the barn. They were always close to the animals, and it was very smelly.

Houses didn't always have central heating like they do today. They used to be kept warm with an indoor fireplace and the smoke escaped through a chimney pipe.

Before cars were invented, horses were the way to travel. Most families would own horses to get around. They also helped out on the farm pulling heavy wagons.

Houses didn't have indoor toilets or running water. You had to go outside to a smelly shed to do your stinky business in a bucket.

The waste from the outhouse would be gathered every week in a wagon and either dumped in rivers or used as manure for crops. Yuck!

Lots of families would be so packed into a small space that they would send some of their children off to live with relatives who had bigger houses.

FRANCIS TAKES TO THE SEAS

Francis' uncle, William Hawkins, was a privateer*. He loved to hear his uncle's tales of wild sea adventures. When he was a teenager, he went off to be an apprentice on a merchant ship as a navigator**. He was very good at it, quickly learning the skills he needed. Eventually, he was hired along with his two cousins John and William Jr. and joined them as privateers. Later, he was even given his own ship and crew to manage.

*A privateer was like a pirate who worked for the Queen of England. They would still capture merchant ships and steal loot, but they would give a cut of the bounty to the Queen's court, so she let them do it without punishment.

**A navigator would have learned skills like how to spot signs of a storm, how to read maps, how to use navigational devices, and how to use the stars to locate where you were in the world.

—THE SLAVE TRADE—

Now, you probably think of pirates stealing chests full of gold and jewels, but Frances stole people. Back then, privateers used to travel to Africa and steal people from their beds, kidnapping them and taking them on huge boats to the New World to sell as slaves.

The slave trade was a horrible business. Treating people like property and buying, selling and stealing them is a vile and outrageous thing, but it was very common back then. Greedy people can do some terrible, evil things for money sometimes!

A continent that the Europeans found and stole from its natives, called America.

What's the New World?

Francis took all the people he stole (or at least, all the people who survived the unhygienic and dangerous boat trip) to the Spanish Colonies in the new world and tried to sell them for lots of gold. The Spanish said no because they didn't like the English very much. So, Francis and his crew set their towns on fire and threatened them with pistols. The Spanish settlers reluctantly agreed to do business with them, even if it made the King of Spain quite angry.

4

HOW TO BE A NAVIGATOR

Back then, sailors didn't have GPS like we do now to navigate. They had to use tools, such as a compass, a quadrant, an astrolabe, and a map.

Boys as young as eight years old would be taken aboard full time to learn the ropes in exchange for manual labor. And you think school is bad . . .

Compass

Uses the earth's magnetic pull to always point north. The design on this compass face is called a compass rose. It shows north, east, south, and west, and sometimes has numbered angles around the edge. People could use it to make sure they are heading in the correct direction. Compasses are still used today!

Astrolabe

Used to measure the angle between the horizon and either the sun in the daytime or the North Star at night. Because the earth is round, sailors could find how far they were from the equator by the distance between the horizon and the star. The word astrolabe is Latin for star taker. Historians think they've been around for over 2,000 years.

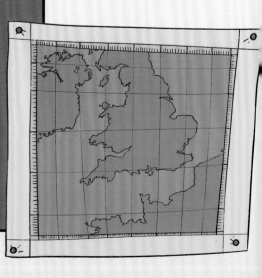

Quadrant and Octant

The quadrant got its name because it is one-fourth of a full circle, and the word quad means four. It was used to measure the height of either the North Star or the sun. Many years later, the octant was invented, it was like an upgraded quadrant using mirrors and an eyepiece.

Map

Map makers are called cartographers. Maps would have vertical lines (latitude) and horizontal lines (longitude) across them. People can use the latitude and longitude together to mark a unique point on the map.

5

PIRATE PERILS

Being a privateer meant plundering foreign ships to steal their treasure. The English called this privateering because they didn't consider it piracy to steal from countries they didn't like. Just because the Queen said it was okay didn't mean that the other sailors were going to give up their loot without a fight! Drake and his men had to face off against swords, guns, and even cannons!

Can you find the hidden treasure on this ship without running into trouble?

FRANCIS AND THE SPANISH

Damnations! Traitors!!

One time in 1568, the fleet of Francis and his cousin John had to make a pit stop in the Spanish harbor of San Juan de Ulúa to repair their ships and gather supplies for the journey ahead. But stopping in a Spanish port was dangerous, especially when 13 Spanish war ships docked just after them. John managed to make a deal with them. The English ships wouldn't cause any trouble; they'd just fix up their ships and leave, and the Spanish soldiers would leave them alone in return. It seemed like a safe agreement, but the Spanish betrayed them. Francis, John, and their fleet were attacked without warning by hundreds of soldiers. They were outnumbered and outmatched. Before they could escape, 500 of their men were killed. After that, Francis hated the Spanish a lot.

Francis ignored orders to help out and his ship was the first to run away and sail back to England. John and only 14 of his men came back alive, and he wasn't so happy with Francis for leaving him.

Francis wanted revenge on the Spanish, so he and his crew thieved from them whenever they could. He even ran a mule train heist, led by a group of Cimarrones*. Francis and his men hid out in the forests near the Spanish colonies. Spanish soldiers were transporting gold and silver on mules through the forest, and the Cimarrones told Francis where to find their route. They attacked the soldiers and stole the treasure!

* The Cimarrones were a group of African slaves who escaped their Spanish oppressors. They hated the Spanish even more than Drake did and had lots of inside knowledge.

Eek!

When Francis and his men ran to shore with their treasures, their ship was gone! Thinking on his feet, Francis ordered them to build a raft, and they drifted to the nearest island. Luckily, the ship had just been hiding from the Spanish and sailed by the next day to pick them up!

Monarchy madness

The King of Spain, Phillip II, hated Francis so much that he wrote to the Queen of England, asking her to punish Francis for his crimes. Spain had been sending out explorers to claim parts of the new world, gathering treasures and spices from lands unknown. At that time Spain was far richer and more powerful than England. So the Queen, Elizabeth I, agreed in order to avoid a war. Francis was asked to visit the Queen's court.

He was very afraid, though; the Queen was well known for chopping off people's heads, and he rather liked his head attached to his body.

But instead of punishing him, the Queen tasked him with a secret mission. She was jealous of Spain, so she gave him a whole fleet of ships and told him to travel to the new world and bring her back riches and treasures.

THE SPICE TRADE

Europe had recently discovered that they could trade with other countries in the East for wonderful spices. Some of the spices they traded for included: cinnamon (Sri Lanka), cloves (Indonesia), nutmeg (Indonesia), ginger (Southeast Asia), mace (Indonesia), pepper (Southeast Asia), cubeb (Indonesia), galangal (Southern Asia), anise (Southwest Asia), cardamom (Indonesia), cumin (Middle East), and saffron (India).

Can you find the following spices below?

Cinnamon

Cloves

Nutmeg

Mace

Pepper

Cardamom

Cumin

Saffron

THE SHIP

The fleet had five ships with 170 men aboard (an awful lot of pirates . . . erm, I mean privateers). The main ship of the fleet was called the Pelican.

The Great Cabin: *The captain's comfortable private quarters*

Armory: *Where the weapons and armor for battles are kept*

The Gun Deck: *A whole deck with cannons lined up on each side to blow holes in passing ships*

But to flatter a rich and powerful man called Christopher Hatton, whose coat of arms was a golden deer,

Francis renamed the main ship to The Golden Hind later. He even got someone to carve a wooden hind for the front of the ship!

One man aboard was Thomas Doughty. Francis really didn't like him, thinking he was a mutineer*! He was so paranoid about being betrayed that he got rid of Thomas (in a rather nasty, pirate-y way!). The problem was, Thomas was actually good friends with Christopher Hatton. Whoops! That's why Francis had to flatter Christopher.

*Mutineer is a shipmate who refuses to take orders and sometimes tries to turn the crew against their captain.

Fo'c'sle/Forecastle: *The sailors' living quarters*

The Hold: *A huge room to keep enough food and supplies for everyone on board for weeks at a time, as well as any treasures they collect*

The Brig: *Jail for naughty pirates*

Ballast: *The bottom of the ship was full of heavy rocks to keep it upright*

DESPERATE TIMES CALL FOR DESPERATE MEASURES

Early in their journey, Francis and his crew were stuck in a storm for TWO MONTHS, and in that time, they ran very low on their provisions. Hungry and desperate, they hunted and ate penguins! Well . . . not exactly. Around the North Atlantic existed a species of bird called the great auks. They looked a lot like penguins: fat, flightless, black and white birds that Drake and his crew would herd onto the ship by planks for an easy meal.

Great auks were so slow and easy to catch that people ate them into extinction, and they can no longer be seen today.

Great Auk

Poor birds! I'm glad I can fly.

TROUBLED WATERS AHEAD

When passing the Atlantic Ocean, Francis lost two ships in a storm: Swan and Christopher. After passing the Magellan Strait, he got caught by another storm and lost the Elizabeth and the Marigold, leaving only the Golden Hind to complete the journey.

When the stormed calmed, Francis continued forward, sailing north towards the coast of Peru into waters that were filled with Spanish ships.

Eek! Watch out!

NO CALM AFTER THE STORM

They sailed further and further north to the Mocha Islands where the local residents, called the Mapuche, attacked them, thinking they were the Spanish. Francis and most of his crew escaped alive, but the entire crew got a terrible beating, so they continued to flee north.

Not that they didn't deserve it, the rotten lot.

The Mapuche didn't like the Spanish already because they were invaders who were trying to get rid of the Mapuche. The Spanish wanted their homes and their gold and didn't approve of their religion. Spanish soldiers had been attacking and torturing the Mapuche people ever since they arrived. The Mapuche were strong and determined, and they fought hard for their freedom and independence. Even if they'd known that Francis and his men weren't Spanish, they probably wouldn't have liked them anyway because Francis was up to the same nasty deeds, trying to steal things that didn't belong to him.

15

THE TREASURES OF THE CACAFUEGO

Francis soon heard about a Spanish treasure ship up ahead called Nuestra Señora de la Concepción (later given the rude name Cacafuego by the English, which means fire-pooper) and went to steal from it. There had never been English privateers in the Pacific Ocean before, so the Spanish weren't expecting the attack at all! Despite attacking the ship and stealing their loot, Francis treated the Spanish sailors surprisingly well this time. After wounding the captain, San Juan De Anton, Francis helped him clean the injury. He also let the crew walk away unharmed, even giving them each some money to take with them. It seemed he WAS having a very good day.

Francis and his crew stole 79 pounds of gold! That's the same weight as 36 pineapples!

And 26 TONS of silver bars! That's the same weight as four T-rexes!

As well as 12 chests of silver coins, piles of jewels, and a solid gold crucifix!

In today's money, what they stole would be worth around 60,000,000 dollars! Think of all the cool things you could buy with it! I'd buy a castle made of bird seed.

FINDERS KEEPERS: NOVA ALBION

They sailed all the way up around North America. It suddenly got stormy, and the Golden Hind started to leak, so they stopped on a beach for repairs. Drake named that place Nova Albion, which is Latin for New England and claimed the land in the name of the Queen, even though it didn't really belong to him or the Queen.

Nova Albion

Pirates did that kind of thing a lot . . . actually, so did the English.

The place Francis claimed is called California today! So why is it known as California rather than Nova Albion? Well, Spanish settlers had actually arrived there before Drake had. In Spain, there was a well-known romance book called *Las Sergas de Esplandian* by Garci Rodriguez de Montalvo, featuring a mythical island called California. The Spanish explorers thought the had actually found the island from the book, so they named it as such.

THE NOTORIOUS NORTHWEST PASSAGE

Northwest Passage

Brrrr!

Eek!

Go get then!

Drake's route

Francis wanted to take a short route home by sailing up around the top of North America to loop back towards England, a route called the Northwest Passage. No one really knew if this route even existed. Francis never found it and decided that it either must be made up or too far north for humans to travel safely due to the cold. To make things worse, the Spanish ships in these waters were hunting them down fast.

So Francis, with lack of alternative options, made a brave decision for them to be the first English sailors to cross the Pacific Ocean. His plan was to sail around the whole globe to go back to England!

What Francis didn't know back then was that the Northwest Passage actually does exist! It is a dangerous route to sail because of the cold, so it wasn't discovered until the 1850s by an Irish explorer called Robert McClure, and even then, no one completed the journey until 1903 when Norwegian sailor Roald Amundsen crossed it – over 300 years after Francis!

SICKENING AND SALTY SAILORS' SNACKS

Imagine being stuck on a smelly boat for that long. Yuck! Good thing they didn't get seasick!

Maggoty Biscuits: Dry baked biscuits were brought along because they lasted for years, but they would often be infested with maggots. You could bang them on the table to knock the bugs out before eating them. Eww!

Salted Meat: Dried and salted meat would keep because the salt preserved it. It was hard, chewy, salty, and left you feeling very thirsty after.

Seafood: Whatever fish the sailors could catch, they would cook and eat. Turtles were often gathered from the beach for a hearty meal whenever they went ashore.

They escaped the Spanish ships and ended up sailing west for 68 days. What a trek! They were low on supplies, and there were no fridges back then, so the only food they had was things that wouldn't go bad. No fruit or vegetables in sight! With the lack of vitamin C from fruit and vegetables, an illness called scurvy was common to sailors. It made their bones achy and their gums diseased. Remember that next time you try to hide that orange in your lunch box.

YE OLD WORLD

Well, before we had cars and planes, people had to travel by horse and boat. It took a really long time and was often very dangerous. Since travel was so hard, not many people knew what the world looked like and sort of had to guess a lot of parts. Because of this, the world map looked pretty different back then to the way it does today.

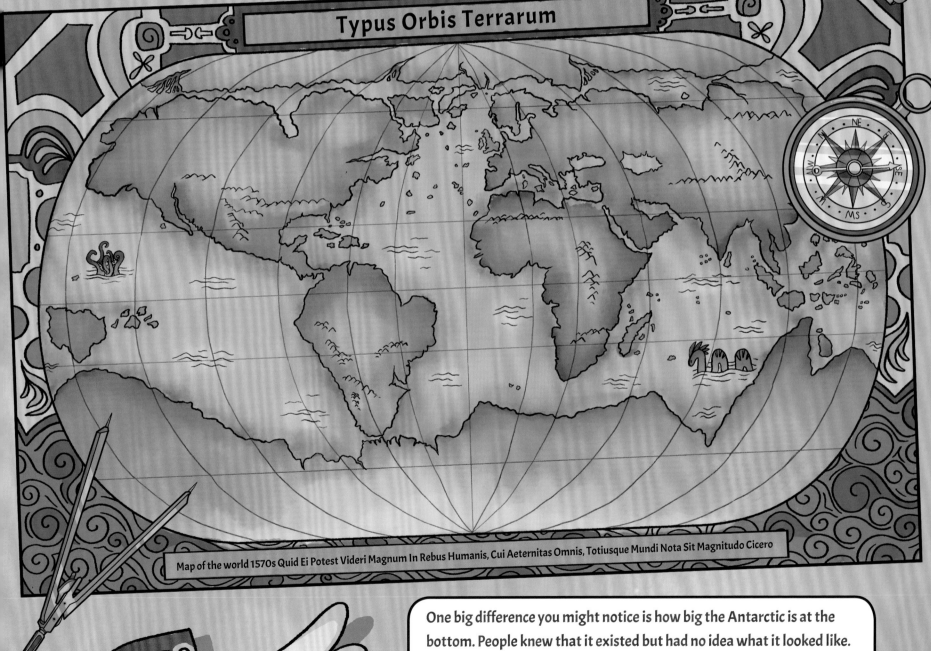

Typus Orbis Terrarum

Map of the world 1570s Quid Ei Potest Videri Magnum In Rebus Humanis, Cui Aeternitas Omnis, Totiusque Mundi Nota Sit Magnitudo Cicero

One big difference you might notice is how big the Antarctic is at the bottom. People knew that it existed but had no idea what it looked like. It was often called Terra Australis Incognita, which is Latin for 'unknown land of the south' and would cover the whole bottom of the map because people assumed it was huge.

SPICES AND SULTANS

Francis and his crew sailed all the way to the Philippines, then to the Maluku Islands. They saw fascinating things no English sailors had ever seen before, like crabs that climb trees and strange trees bearing fruit they'd never seen.

21

The Canarium Vulgare, or 'java almond', is one fruit they came across in Indonesia. It comes from a tree that grows clusters of alien-looking pods that have edible seeds inside that are similar to a regular almond, just a bit sweeter.

It was quite a party when they arrived! Babu put on a show to greet them with canoes rowing in unison to drum beats and lines of warriors dressed to the nines. Francis, being a bit of a show-off, had an orchestra on his ship play songs while they fired cannons in salute. It was very loud and exciting!

Luckily, they didn't need to rely on mysterious fruits, as they soon arrived on an island and met Sultan Babu, who ruled the Sultanate of Ternate. He had also been fighting with the Spanish for years and took an immediate liking to Francis, so he prepared him and his crew a huge feast. Babu was very rich in a spice called cloves, which Europe was crazy for. Francis made a deal with the Sultan, trading some armor and a gold ring for SIX TONS of cloves. What a deal!

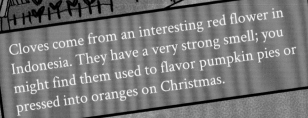

Cloves come from an interesting red flower in Indonesia. They have a very strong smell; you might find them used to flavor pumpkin pies or pressed into oranges on Christmas.

A CATASTROPHIC CLOVE CONUNDRUM!

The ship was so heavy with treasure (and cloves) that it got stuck on a coral reef. Francis was worried they'd never get free and would perish once they ran out of food. The crew had to throw eight of their canons and three tons of cloves overboard to try to get unstuck. Thankfully, it worked; otherwise, they'd have been in real trouble.

NOOO! MY CLOVES!

What a waste. I'd have thrown Drake overboard instead. I'm sure his ego weighs more than all the canons and cloves combined.

HOMEWARD BOUND! (AT LAST)

They finally sailed home across the Indian ocean, but only 56 of the sailors survived the full voyage out of the 170 who left! (The life of a sailor is a treacherous one!) They docked at Plymouth in 1580 and were met with country-wide celebration.

Can you help them navigate their way back without getting into trouble?

A KNIGHTED NUTCASE

When they finally arrived in England, they were hailed as heroes. The Queen even knighted Francis. Knighting is where the Queen touches your shoulders with a sword and then you get the title 'Sir' rather than Mr. It's only given to people who have done a huge service to their country. Women can be knighted, too, but it's called damehood instead. They get the title 'Dame' instead of Mrs./Miss/Ms. People are still being knighted even today!

RICH, FAMOUS, AND READY TO REST

Francis gave around £47,000 to the Queen and was allowed to keep around £10,000 for himself. He brought a huge estate to live on near his hometown. Now that his great journey was over, he'd retire and live out his days with his wife on land in peace and luxury.

Thank goodness. Is his reign of terror finally over?

The King of Spain was still furious with Francis and pretty mad with England in general. A war broke out, and the Queen asked Francis to lead the fight. In July of 1558, lines of ships two miles wide sailed out. The English and Spanish ships battled for days . . .

FiRE POWER!

Then, Francis commanded the soldiers to set eight of their empty ships on fire and send them out towards where the Spanish ships were anchored.

What is with this man and fire?

The Spanish didn't want the fire spreading to their ships. They sailed away and lost formation, which made them much more vulnerable to the English cannons. It was a dangerous and crazy plan, but it worked, and the battle was soon won!

28

ONE FINAL EXPEDITION

In 1595, Francis had his very last voyage. He convinced the Queen to let him take an expedition to the Caribbean. Francis, joined by his cousin John Hawkins, and their fleet of 27 ships set off, but things didn't quite go to plan . . .

His cousin died of a disease on the way. It hit Francis hard; he started to feel quite lonely and old. At 54 years old, Francis began to wonder how much longer he himself had left.

Do I have wrinkles like that? Yikes.

Then, they tried to attack some Spanish ships, but this time, the Spanish were prepared. Francis and his men were pushed back.

THEN, a horrible illness called dysentery crept into their ship, and the crew got very sick.

Just when he thought it couldn't get any worse, Francis caught it too and got very ill.

DAMNATIONS! WHERE'S THE PRIVY?!

GOODBYE FRANCIS!

On January 28th, 1596, he demanded that his crew help him out of bed and dress him in his armor, ready for battle. He laid back down in his battle gear and passed away one hour later.

The crew put him in a lead-lined coffin and buried him at sea, which was respectful for a sailor. They played trumpets and blew the cannons loudly as he slid into the ocean and disappeared forever.

Francis was gone, and the news spread worldwide.

Spain celebrated;

Francis Drake was only the second person in the world to sail the globe, but his story is still being told hundreds of years later. It just goes to show that you don't have to be the first at something to make history.

England mourned.

Drake's Drum: Drake's Drum is a drum that Francis took with him on his world journey. He had the drum sent to Buckland Abbey and vowed that if England were ever in danger and someone was to beat the drum, he would return from the dead to defend the country. Spooky!

FERDINAND

- A Portuguese captain sailing on behalf of Spain.

- Grew up part of an upper-class family.

- Made his circumnavigation of the earth between 1519 to 1522 and died before getting home.

- Was the first person to attempt to travel the circumference of the whole world.

- When a mutiny broke out, some of his crew stole three of his ships, but Ferdinand and his supporters won the fight.

- Was killed in the Battle of Mactan, a fight that took place because Ferdinand wanted to convert the local tribes to Christianity, and one of the chiefs, called Lapulapu, refused.

- Only 18 surviving members of Ferdinand's crew made it home out of 270.

- His journey showed that it was possible to travel from Spain to the Spice Islands without traveling around Africa and later helped prove that the earth was round.

• FRANCIS •

• An English privateer sailing on behalf of England.

• Grew up part of a middle-class family.

• Made his circumnavigation of the earth between 1577 and 1580 and survived the trip.

• Was the second person to attempt to travel the circumference of the whole world.

• Avoided a mutiny by having Thomas Doughty killed when he had suspicions that he was against him.

• Was killed by dysentery, a disease caused by dirty water, likely from the poor hygiene conditions on the ship.

• 56 out of 170 surviving members of Francis's crew made it around the world and back alive.

• His journey made a lot of money for England and a lot of trouble for Spain. It gave England a larger part in the spice trade, made Francis very famous, and brought back new knowledge about the far reaches of the globe!

THE SPICE TRADE

Europe had recently discovered that they could trade with other countries in the East for wonderful spices. Some of the spices they traded for included: cinnamon (Sri Lanka), cloves (Indonesia), nutmeg (Indonesia), ginger (Southeast Asia), mace (Indonesia), pepper (Southeast Asia), cubeb (Indonesia), galangal (Southern Asia), anise (Southwest Asia), cardamom (Indonesia), cumin (Middle East), and saffron (India).

Can you find the following spices below?

Cinnamon
Cloves
Nutmeg
Mace
Pepper
Cardamom
Cumin
Saffron

HOMEWARD BOUND! (AT LAST)

They finally sailed home across the Indian ocean, but only 56 of the sailors survived the full voyage out of the 170 who left! (The life of a sailor is a treacherous one!) They docked at Plymouth in 1580 and were met with country-wide celebration.

Can you help them navigate their way back without getting into trouble?

24

PUZZLE ANSWERS

PIRATE PERILS

Being a privateer meant plundering foreign ships to steal their treasure. The English called this privateering because they didn't consider it piracy to steal from countries they didn't like. Just because the Queen said it was okay didn't mean that the other sailors were going to give up their loot without a fight! Drake and his men had to face off against swords, guns, and even cannons!

Can you find the hidden treasure on this ship without running into trouble?

6

How many did you solve?

The wacky, the funny, and the eccentric, the second ones in the world . . .

The Second in the World
to Sail the Globe: Sir Fransic Drake

Sir Francis Drake, a murderous pirate working for the Queen of England in the 16th century, was the second person ever known to sail around the globe. On a quest to steal treasures, hunt for spices, and annoy the King of Spain as much as possible, Francis and his crew aboard the Golden Hind might not have been the first, but they were certainly the wackiest.

The Second in the World
to Discover Evolution: Alfred Russel Wallace

Alfred Russel Wallace, a 19th-century naturalist, was the second person in the world known to discover the secrets of evolution. With his epic journey around the world in search of creepy crawlies and flying beasties, firey ship disasters, and feverish forest findings, Alfred, with the help of his little apprentice Ali, might not have been the first, but he was certainly the most fun.

The Second in the World
to Invent the Telephone: Elisha Gray

Elisha Gray, a dairy farmer turned inventor in the 19th century, came second in the race to invent the telephone (or did he ?). With his wacky discoveries using bathtub instruments, rich dentists, and electric pianos, Elisha might not have been the first, but the story of his discovery is just as eccentric topped off with a mountain of envy.

NEW BOOKS FROM YEEHOO PRESS

Chameleon Can Be

The Happiest Kid

My Monsterpiece

When I'm Not Looking

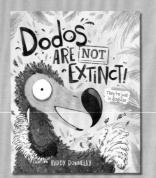

Dodos Are Not Extinct

The Vanishing Lake

The Gentle Bulldozer

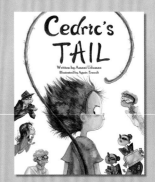

Cedric's Tail

Piper And Purpa Forever!

The Whole World Inside Nan's Soup

Milo's Moonlight Mission

The Perfect Party

Masha Munching

The School of Failure: A Story About Success

Who Is It, Whoodini?